"*On Homesickness* is a masterful meditation on nostalgia, founded in the tender device of riffs on the 120 counties of the Commonwealth of Kentucky. For this Kentucky native the device is so obvious that it borders on genius, because what is genius but incarnating in art the beauty in the details everyone else has taken for granted? My first thought on opening it was: Why didn't I think of that?–a sure sign the author is onto something sweet. The riffs are lyrical, poignant, evocative–they call to mind Vladimir Nabokov, our high priest of nostalgia. Everyone who has left home, any home, anywhere, will want to read these, for a sobering assessment of why you left–along with all those who remained, for an equally rich assessment of the price of staying put."

–Fenton Johnson, author of *The Man Who Loved Birds*

"In his ambitious and elegant long essay, Jesse Donaldson, modern day voyager, passionately wrestles with the question of home: Where is home, how is a home imagined, why do we leave, and how might we (do we want to?) return? Donaldson sets out to root himself far from his origins, and finds himself beckoned back, in surprising and unsettling ways. At turns strict and indulgent, bold and resigned, he fearlessly questions the conventional terms of nostalgia, and finds it to be both a constructed fantasy, and as sharply real as Kentucky bluegrass. Certainties emerge from such rigorous internal voyaging: love roots us in. Children root us in. Places in our past will hold out their hands in temptation and reproach, in friendship and with patience while we find our way back–if we're lucky enough to hail from land that loves us, and that kindled our deepest longings."

–Lia Purpura, author of *Rough Likeness*

IN PLACE

Jeremy Jones, Series Editor

Elena Passarello, Series Editor

On Homesickness

A PLEA

JESSE DONALDSON

VANDALIA PRESS / MORGANTOWN 2017

First edition published 2017 by West Virginia University Press
Printed in the United States of America

ISBN:

paper	978-1-946684-00-4
epub	978-1-946684-01-1
pdf	978-1-946684-02-8

Library of Congress Cataloging-in-Publication Data is available
from the Library of Congress

Cover design and interior illustrations by by Danielle Delph.

Art direction and interior design by Than Saffel.

For b., without whom nothing would be possible

KENTUCKY INDEX

Counties

County	County Seat	County	County Seat
Adair	Columbia	Knott	Hindman
Allen	Scottsville	Knox	Barbourville
Anderson	Lawrenceburg	Larue	Hodgenville
Ballard	Wickliffe	Laurel	London
Barren	Glasgow	Lawrence	Louisa
Bath	Owingsville	Lee	Beattyville
Bell	Pineville	Leslie	Hyden
Boone	Burlington	Letcher	Whitesburg
Bourbon	Paris	Lewis	Vanceburg
Boyd	Catlettsburg	Lincoln	Stanford
Boyle	Danville	Livingston	Smithland
Bracken	Brooksville	Logan	Russellville
Breathitt	Jackson	Lyon	Eddyville
Breckinridge	Hardinsburg	McCracken	Paducah
Bullitt	Shepherdsville	McCreary	Whitley City
Butler	Morgantown	McLean	Calhoun
Caldwell	Princeton	Madison	Richmond
Calloway	Murray	Magoffin	Salyersville
Campbell	Alexandria	Marion	Lebanon
	Newport	Marshall	Benton
Carlisle	Bardwell	Martin	Inez
Carroll	Carrollton	Mason	Maysville
Carter	Grayson	Meade	Brandenburg
Casey	Liberty	Menifee	Frenchburg
Christian	Hopkinsville	Mercer	Harrodsburg
Clark	Winchester	Metcalfe	Edmonton
Clay	Manchester	Monroe	Tompkinsville
Clinton	Albany	Montgomery	Mt. Sterling
Crittenden	Marion	Morgan	West Liberty
Cumberland	Burkesville	Muhlenberg	Greenville
Daviess	Owensboro	Nelson	Bardstown
Edmonson	Brownsville	Nicholas	Carlisle
Elliott	Sandy Hook	Ohio	Hartford
Estill	Irvine	Oldham	LaGrange
Fayette	Lexington	Owen	Owenton
Fleming	Flemingsburg	Owsley	Booneville
Floyd	Prestonsburg	Pendleton	Falmouth
Franklin	Frankfort	Perry	Hazard
Fulton	Hickman	Pike	Pikeville
Gallatin	Warsaw	Powell	Stanton
Garrard	Lancaster	Pulaski	Somerset
Grant	Williamstown	Robertson	Mt. Olivet
Graves	Mayfield	Rockcastle	Mt. Vernon
Grayson	Leitchfield	Rowan	Morehead
Green	Greensburg	Russell	Jamestown
Greenup	Greenup	Scott	Georgetown
Hancock	Hawesville	Shelby	Shelbyville
Hardin	Elizabethtown	Simpson	Franklin
Harlan	Harlan	Spencer	Taylorsville
Harrison	Cynthiana	Taylor	Campbellsville
Hart	Munfordville	Todd	Elkton
Henderson	Henderson	Trigg	Cadiz
Henry	New Castle	Trimble	Bedford
Hickman	Clinton	Union	Morganfield
Hopkins	Madisonville	Warren	Bowling Green
Jackson	McKee	Washington	Springfield
Jefferson	Louisville	Wayne	Monticello
Jessamine	Nicholasville	Webster	Dixon
Johnson	Paintsville	Whitley	Williamsburg
Kenton	Covington	Wolfe	Campton
	Independence	Woodford	Versailles

To Springfield, To Jefferson City, To Wentzville, To Kansas City.

It begins as a lump in the throat, a sense of wrong,
a homesickness, a lovesickness . . .

–Robert Frost

Jefferson County

1780

They came as Virginians, shed their airs, and made this land their own. They came floating flatboats and blazing dense woods. They came to sleep under constellated night until they found holler home, sheltered themselves inside cabins built along creeks that spread out from the Ohio, settled the banks of the Beargrass and Goose. They sought freedom from a governor who levied taxes but offered nothing in return, a man not unlike the monarch they'd fought to depose. They were a rough-and-tumble pack, prone to violence. Unbridled. Clannish by nature. Men and women who crossed mountains for solitude. Rumor spread that the Indian word from which their new home took its name meant "dark and bloody ground" but it did not. Kentucke. Kentacke. Kentucky. Meadowland. Grassyland. The place where I was born.

Lincoln County

1780

They followed the Athiamiowee, the Warriors' Path, and changed its name to Wilderness Road. The path–which had known only the feet of men and before that only the hooves of creatures–became rutted by wagon wheels bearing the weight of transient lives. I would be lying to you if I said they found Eden. Some found bitter orchards and sulfur springs. Others built forts, which they called stations, and warred with natives from behind thick walls. And the natives–the Shawnee, the Choctaw, and the Cherokee–they suffered. Plagues descended as their hunting grounds were colonized by men quick to raise rifle. In the end, the army of a hostile nation marched them toward the parched deserts of Oklahoma and left their dead along the trail for buzzards and flies. Let this be a warning, then, about how fleeting our homes can be, about how what is lost is often never recovered.

Fayette County

1780

You and I live in Oregon now, and outside our window yellow-orange cosmos bloom–the seeds of which were given to us by my mother in Kentucky. We tossed them from our car windows as we headed west–cosmos dotting the neglected hell strips of Great Plains gas stations and diners. I scattered the last seeds in our garden the year we arrived and left things to chance. Do you remember carrying cosmos down the aisle? We didn't know it then, but cosmos are named for their symmetry, for their balance, like the way you balance me and I you. A universe in order. In my vows, I stole a bit from Whitman. I said, To me, you are a cosmos. So when I look at the flowers outside our window, I think of both you and Kentucky. And there's the discord. A divided loyalty. Perhaps one day we will follow the cosmos back, drive east over the divide and into the rising sun, reverse course across the plains. I will glance passenger-side and see a cosmos searching for cosmos that point the way home. And yet I realize this is not likely: life takes from us the places we've known and we rarely return to root ourselves a second time.

Nelson County

1785

Even the most accomplished livers die carrying some untapped longing. Perhaps this is why ghosts choose to linger. And if my haunting grounds are the bluegrass, then I am not the first. Come: let me buy you a drink at the Old Talbott, where the spirit of Jesse James prowls the halls beside an unnamed lady in white. Take my hand so I can run your fingers over the bullet-riddled walls where Jesse emptied his pistol shooting butterflies. The outlaw's legend I can tell you, but the lady in white remains a mystery. Perhaps she, too, was led here by someone she trusted. Perhaps she found herself trapped. Come: let's warm ourselves by the fire. After midnight we can lurk in shadows and wait until the guests are alone and vulnerable. We can push the perched glass from its shelf and tinkle the keys of the piano long after the player has left. We can spend an eternity here: me, a man who shoots butterflies, and you, a lady in white.

Bourbon County

1786

If an eternity is too long, then let me at least whisk you to Paris. There we can dine on hot browns and raise a glass of the county's nom de plume. I'll regale you with stories about how this place was once called Hopewell (named by optimistic Virginians), and we will mock our aristocratic neighbors in Richmond and Roanoke with their tête-à-têtes in gay Par-ee. And after dinner's last cigarette, we will stomp beneath the eaves of the tobacco barn until the sun rises over our little slice of France, which at least one of us will christen "Pairs."

Mercer County

1786

Do you remember the weekend we spent on Pleasant Hill? The Shakers–who once lived here–understood the complex patterns of harmony and arranged them in divine proportion. Before they raised houses, they made tools–each pin planed to fit the augur's hole, each beam set with plumb level and Jacob's staff. Their unmortared fences required only the patience to find the right stone. I keep asking you to move to Kentucky, but what if your stone doesn't stack? Sometimes I feel like an impatient child who hasn't learned the difference between square and round pegs. I bang away and bang away–hoping divine proportion is a trinity of you, me, and Kentucky–but what if each hammer strike merely rings out in discord?

Madison County

1786

I returned to Kentucky once without you, took a job teaching college students how to compose rhetorically. You were in Houston studying poetry and translating dead languages. We didn't say it then, but our parting was a standoff of sorts. A great siege of space and time. Neither of us had ever asked the other to sacrifice and now we both asked once. Come. Follow me. Before those months apart I'd understood synecdoche only as an idea and never a feeling. I was at home in Kentucky, but you weren't there. Then I came running to you in Texas and I was whole but I wasn't home. And thus a rift formed–between the limestone banks of place and love–a tributary of doubt with no Charon to help me cross. On one side you, my lady in white. On the other Kentucky, my dark lady.

Mason County

1789

Perhaps this makes me a river, which is a muddy metaphor but apt. Since leaving Kentucky, my life has been defined by movement. For years I considered myself a happy "wanderer," a word we took from the Germans, whose definition isn't about aimless movement so much as communing with nature (to *wandern* or hike). I treated Kentucky as a safe haven, returning only to eat a homemade meal and sleep in a comfortable bed. But something changed as I drifted from state to state and town to town. Perhaps I grew tired. Perhaps I grew bored. Though it's more likely the change happened when I met you. I felt a need to know where you stood, to stand beside, to hold and steady. Lord, steady.

Woodford County

1789

The Germans have another term that might shed light on the situation, though *Sehnsucht* is difficult to translate. It's compounded from *das Sehnen,* a deep yearning, and die Sucht, addiction. A psychologist from the Max Planck Institutes describes *Sehnsucht* as "intense desires for ideal states of life that are remote or unattainable." In this sense, it is a state limited to adulthood and checked imagination. The summer after I learned to drive, I played baseball in Versailles, and each time I sped Highway 60 to practice, I felt the world's embrace. That summer I resolved to watch Kentucky fade in my rearview. I didn't yet know the meaning of the word "remote." I didn't yet know that life made things unattainable. What do I remember of that drive now? That you pass the racecourse and the airport? A donut shop? That an empty castle lay across the county line, built by a man for his wife after they'd honeymooned in Europe? I was at my most sublime on that field. I wish you could have seen me then, so much more the boy who looks ahead than the man who looks behind.

Washington County

1792

It takes time for a people and place to fall in lockstep. Each of the counties I've mentioned were once clay shaped by Virginian hands. Virginia, the older sister who for years deemed young Kentucky a mere province, who knew little of her multitudes, who thought nothing of her cosmos. It wasn't until Kentucky found a people willing to defend her that she carved a county of her own. And that first severing cut must've given her pleasure, because she kept carving and carving and carving until the counties numbered six score, until the scars made constellations across her body. She has always been generous, Kentucky, a motherland to tired itinerants. So come: lie here beside me. I will carve out a spot and call it by your name.

Scott County

1792

Be warned: new beginnings are rarely pure, and neither are the men who seek them. Take Richard Mentor Johnson. It is said he lost his Senate seat and returned to Kentucky because he loved an octoroon named Julia. But what if I told you Johnson had a reputation for graft and back-channeled lucrative government contracts to start a sham Indian academy? Do we celebrate his loyalty concerning matters of the heart or lament his deceit concerning matters of the coin? Which past was Johnson fleeing: his nobility or his fraud? I don't know why I want to flee Oregon, why I feel it so acutely. I never planned to be the sort of man who sought the familiar, who made pleas, but that's the man I've become.

Shelby County

1792

As a child, I dreamed of becoming an adventurer, a headlong blazer of trails, and together you and I can breathe life into those swaggering visions. Climb to the top of Jeptha Knob with me and survey the bluegrass. The lights of Lexington lie east and Louisville west, but tonight we'll sleep beneath the glow of far-off galaxies, just as Daniel and his Rebecca did. I have only my arms to protect you, so we'll have to trust in the charity of the land–the warm blanket of night and soft bed of grass, the pillow of pine and protection of stars. Let Cassiopeia order the Archer and Huntsman to shoot a fortress of arrows around our slumbering bodies and keep the dogs at bay. Come morning, I will thatch a roof and cut a door to make our fortress a home–a place where we can start a tribe all our own.

Logan County

1792

If The Knobs don't suit you, then let us steal away to Rogues' Harbor and live among the murderers and thieves. Here, a rogue Jesse James fell in love with his cousin-wife. And here, along the banks of the Red River, a roguish president shot a man dead. You'll find a fine line between right and wrong in Kentucky, for righteousness and rightness rarely go hand in hand. If the preacher/confidence man comes to awaken us from our sins, bite your thumb and sneer. Call him a worthless poltroon. And after he pockets his congregants' last dimes, we will rob his caravan and buy a round for the good, honest criminals of the Harbor.

Clark County

1793

What is just and what is not can't be meted out on scales like gold or sand. There's no simple right and wrong, no moral absolute. Take the life of George Rogers Clark, a hero remembered mostly for falling drunk into a fire and losing his leg. Years before he marched his ragged band of two hundred through the swollen streams of wet winter to capture Fort Vincennes. And so what if his men suspected Clark was intoxicated the entire campaign? They adored him. Clark had borrowed money to keep them fed and clothed even after the governor of Virginia turned his back. When the war ended, Clark set to marry his intended, a Spanish beauty named Teresa, but his debts came due, and in an ill-fated scheme to pay his creditors, he accepted the fraudulent title: Commander-in-Chief of the French Revolutionary Legion on the Mississippi River. His debt only grew. Clark's final days will break your heart. Peglegged and hiccupping. Half-blind from cheap booze, writing crooked letters to the love he lost years before, the woman living out her life at a convent in Spain, her beauty folded inside a simple white habit.

Hardin County

1793

Compare the fate of heroic Clark to Philip Arnold, who faked the discovery of a diamond mine. Arnold convinced George McClellan, Charles Tiffany, and Horace Greeley to invest, but who in Kentucky cares that he stole from the barons of the Gilded Age? With his spoils, Arnold bought his wife a two-story outside Elizabethtown. Deeded it in her name. We shouldn't judge a man's actions without taking into account his intentions. Before the diamond scam, Arnold scraped together a living in the dust of western mines. Marooned beneath the forbidding peaks of the Rockies, he managed to find a way home to Mary. I'm not sure how to define what or who is noble, but I do know that even a con man needs a partner.

Green County

1793

My point is this: no man or woman is beyond either reproach or empathy. I don't know whether my preoccupations with Kentucky deserve your empathy or your reproach, if I'm the confidence man or if I'm being conned. All I know is that the dark lady beckons. She slips between us as we sleep and whispers in my ear, intoxicates me with tales of utopia while you lie unperturbed. She fills me with hope–a twenty-pound cyst of hope.

Harrison County

1794

Maybe the dark lady preys on my anxieties. Or maybe she's a seer calling me back where I belong. Or maybe I'm just a means for her to get you to Kentucky. Maybe you are the prize and we are meant to build a family where we have family. My ancestors are scattered ash, and while there is a certain beauty in this, it isn't one I can stand before and bear witness. Outside Cynthiana, you pass a generous graveyard. As a kid, I held my breath whenever we drove by, but no matter how hard I tried, my lungs couldn't carry its length. The superstition holds that by holding your breath you keep the dead from entering the body. It is the sort of belief that only makes sense before you've stood at the foot of a headstone, before you've said some prayer to some God you may not believe in about some soul you're not sure exists. I still hold my breath when I pass cemeteries–not out of fear or superstition, but out of some misplaced solidarity.

Franklin County

1795

My parents, my sisters: they are not dead but they are ghosts. They bounce around the chambers of heart and mind. Eight octagonal halls of echo. Their voices leave tin sounds on my voicemail as though they are calling out over the vale of the Elkhorn, pushing us farther apart than if they'd never reached out at all. I don't want to connect only through emails and cards sent at Christmas, through favorited photos and emoji texts. Maybe it's clannish–the caveman inside me–or maybe it's regret over what I've failed to appreciate. Carson McCullers said of homesickness: "The emotion is Janus-faced: we are torn between a nostalgia for the familiar and an urge for the foreign and strange. As often as not, we are homesick most for the places we have never known." I would add the word "truly." We are homesick most for the places we have never *truly* known.

Campbell County

1795

It is said that my ancestors in Scotland had a disagreement with the Campbells over a tract of land, and that both clans agreed to resolve it with a race to the summit. The Donaldsons were a lumbering, corpulent sort, and so the race was rigged, but when my ancestor started to lag behind, he unsheathed his broadsword, cut off his arm, and flung it to the top. Bloodied and disfigured, we got our land. This is the history I invite you to hold. The myth I offer. The arm I sacrifice.

Bullitt County

1797

We're told that a famished Esau sold his birthright (the riches of Abraham!) to his brother for lentils and bread. Esau later regretted this since Jacob had tumbled out of the womb grasping for more, but I have no such reservations. I offer you my birthright so that my home might become your home too. My price is a single grain of salt. At the grocery store, I like to hold up the Morton Salt Girl and say, Wars were fought over this. You like to roll your eyes. The truth is we don't track the buffalo to the salt lick anymore, or salt its flesh to keep it for winter. Preservation is less important to us nowadays.

Christian County

1797

Lot's wife turned into a pillar of salt for looking back. So am I already salted? And will the same happen to you if you follow me? To accept an offer of salt is to give yourself in service to another. And to live as the salt of the earth is to preserve it. In the Gospel of Mark, Jesus tells his followers, "have salt in yourselves." And while this might give me comfort were I a proper believer, I don't reserve my longing for God, and I don't yearn for salvation. I carry two psalms in my heart. One I carry for Kentucky:

> *I stretch forth my hands unto thee:*
> *my soul* thirsteth *after thee, as a thirsty land. Selah.*

The other I carry for you:

> *Quicken me after thy lovingkindness;*
> *so shall I keep the testimony of thy mouth.*

Montgomery County

1797

You recently gave me a book that mentions Proteus, the shape-shifting sea god who tells you your fortune if you can clasp to him like a tick. But if you think the most common question asked of Proteus involves either love or death, you're wrong. The most common question is: How do I get home?

Bracken County

1797

I picture Proteus along the muddy banks of the Ohio, shuttered beneath limestone bluffs. (The fossil records here tell story of the great Teays and old, brackish seas.) I see myself wrapping my arms around him to ask the same question so many have asked before. But Proteus rarely answers his supplicants. He shifts into that which most terrifies them, and if they let go, he leaves their question unanswered. And what would Proteus become to frighten me? I see him first as a mirror image containing only the worst parts of myself, and then I see him as you, sad and lost because of me. And are these not themselves mirror images? The only difference being that the first I would abandon while the second, the second I would hold. And I would ask that suffering you not, How do I get home? but rather, How can I help you find your way?

Warren County

1797

Let me be your Virgil. Let me lead you down into Lost River Cave where we can dance around the fire and watch our shadows climb the wall. We can make prehistoric love and wait for visions of the future. Jesse James hid here after kidnapping a doctor to tend to his wounded men, and by the time the authorities descended, pistols drawn and torches blazing, Jesse was gone. Like a ghost. Forever lost and running from terrible deeds. Forever dancing away the night.

Garrard County

1797

The transient life must've taken its toll on Jesse by the end. We all need a place to rest our bones, a cave to call our own. The word that keeps cropping up when I try to explain what I'm seeking is "nostalgia." It was coined in 1688 by Johannes Hofer, a Swiss medical student, who analyzed two patients living away from home for the first time. Both suffered from a lack of appetite, pallor, muscle weakness, and general sadness. Both were sent home to die but recovered once returned to the familiar. I've long medicated my own general sadness in the comfortable must of beer. A few times I've thought I found a temporary Virgil, a guide to a path less wandering, and raised my glass in insincere toast to Carrie Nation and her kind. But in reality, I've just been lost, wallowing in the nameless nameless, waiting for you to find me.

Fleming County

1798

Nostalgia comes from the Greek words *algos* (suffering) and *nostos* (homecoming). Johannes Hofer believed that obsessing over home caused the brain to use up its vital spirits and led to a decline of physical function–the mind's preoccupation leading the body to fail. The diagnosis gained popularity throughout Europe. Each culture seemed to adopt it as its own. *Heimweh. Mal de Corazon. Mal du Pays. Homesickness.* Back then the seas were filled with men seeking riches, the borderlands lined with men fighting wars. Slaves, servants, and wives followed. Displacement ruled the day. Because if men couldn't have home, they would at least have homemakers. Along the Licking River, George Stockton, captured by Indians as a baby, had had trouble reintegrating into polite Virginia society after his release. He sought in Kentucky a refuge, a return to childhood wilderness, but it was time more than place that changed Stockton's world. And he would never recover what was lost.

Pulaski County

1799

Over time, Johannes Hofer's beliefs fell out of favor, and clinicians recategorized nostalgia as a pathology of the mind. Throughout the eighteenth and into the nineteenth centuries, suicides in America were commonly attributed to it. Then the Civil War happened. Americans stopped talking about how they missed the places they'd come from. Emerson claimed "place is nothing" and advised men to "advance on Chaos and the Dark." Homesickness became associated with a weak constitution. And it is true that my daydreams of Kentucky feel weak, that I am not self-reliant. Sometimes it feels as if the very ground I walk on might give way, that beneath the soles of my feet lie sinking streams and craters. And yet every morning I plunge back into our basement–my cave of karst–surrounded by books and maps, writing myself back to the place I was born. Perhaps we Kentuckians have reason to hold on to home more than most.

Pendleton County

1799

As a boy, I was told to be placid in the face of anguish, to be courageous in the face of danger, to step forward when the floodwaters rose and the tornadoes landed. But now I ask myself: Why do men romanticize sacrifice? And why do they ask it of women so freely? Is it merely biblical? I hesitate to cast you as the lamb. The other day you told me about an Internet quiz that matches personality with state. The quiz was based on research published in the *Journal of Personality and Social Psychology*. It said I belong in New Mexico.

Livingston County

1799

You took the same quiz and it said you belong in Georgia and then you joked, It must be 'cause I'm a peach. It made me feel foolish for taking the results personally. I know a quiz can't capture longing or translate the language of the heart, but I wanted it to tell me I belong in the Land Between the Lakes. For decades a team of Dutch scientists has worked to develop the Homesickness Validity Questionnaire, though they've learned it is merely "adequate" in differentiating between homesickness and depression. I suppose research on the subject is destined to end in impasse. Homesickness is an oft-repressed emotion and any study is limited by the fallibility of its subjects. Researchers claim there are trends, though: a high level of neuroticism and a rigid nature, a tendency to be less assertive and more dependent on others. According to one study, "severe homesickness is characterised by lower Self-Directedness and, to a lesser extent, higher Self-Transcendence, a combination [best] described as moody." Touché.

Boone County

1799

There were others who pined for the bluegrass before me, men afflicted by longing. In the fall of 1767, at the age of thirty-three, Daniel Boone stepped foot in Kentucky on a long hunt with his brother Squire. Gigantic herds of buffalo congregated around salt licks. An untamed wilderness beckoned. Boone wrote: "I returned home to my family with a determination to bring them as soon as possible to live in Kentucke, which I esteemed a second paradise, at the risk of my life and fortune."

Henry County

1799

Nearly two hundred years later, Wendell Berry, also in his early thirties, left New York City and bought a homestead in Port Royal, a stone's throw from the tobacco farm where he'd grown up. "I knew I had not escaped Kentucky," he wrote, "and had never really wanted to. I was still writing about it, and had recognized that I would probably need to write about it for the rest of my life. Kentucky was my fate—"

Cumberland County

1799

These two men–the frontiersman and the writer–are mentors of a sort, though I'm hesitant to equate my homesickness with theirs. Boone chose Kentucky before its borders had been set. Berry traces his Kentucky bona fides back two hundred years. I, on the other hand, am the sole native-born of my family, and though my parents have adopted the land as Boone did, our roots are shallow. I left the bluegrass half my life ago, sped away as if chased by wolves, and have returned only briefly since. The house where I grew up has been sold. I will never know its creaky floors again. And yet I feel Kentucky's draw like the thinnest of threads stitched into my heart–unspooled and fastened to a stake sunk into the marrowbone of home. When the wind blows, it tugs, and I turn to look over mountains, plateaus, and rivers–the long gap between here and home.

Gallatin County

1799

Of course my story pales in comparison to Daniel Boone's. I'll not make you bear the sorrows his Rebecca bore. We'll not lose a son to Indian attack. Our daughter will not be kidnapped (nor will I be kidnapped). And should any tragedies befall us—for it is true tragedies that do occur here (steamships colliding, cars crashing, civils warring)—then I'll resign my plea. I'll not ask you to stay through tragedy as Daniel did. In truth, I don't know why his Rebecca stayed. It would be easy to assume it had to do with the era's gender norms, but incorrect. Before Kentucky stole his heart, Boone tried to move his family to Florida—a moment of weakness I'll give no further truck. It was Rebecca who refused to live in the swamps. But why then didn't she put her foot down about Kentucky? Why not after she'd lost a son? Why not after almost losing a daughter? What did she find in these dark woods that stirred her so?

Muhlenberg County

1799

The summer after they married, Wendell Berry asked his wife to nest with him in a cabin along the Kentucky River. "For me," Berry wrote, "that was a happy return. . . . For Tanya, who was hardly a country girl, it was a new kind of place, confronting her with hardships she could not have expected." I wonder if Tanya, who was born in California, dreamed of cities and oceans that summer, if she woke up resenting the muted greens and browns outside her door. I wonder how often she doubted the man she'd married. I have to imagine so much of Berry's life has been filled with disappointment. When the seas overtake the land and the air is too thick to breathe, his words will haunt us. And yet the place he calls home blows the tops off its mountains and gives power plants names like Paradise. Except for in a Tanya, where does a man find satisfaction when the world around him is turning to dust?

Ohio County

1799

For months, thoughts about Kentucky have consumed me. Outside, summer is ending and the cosmos are going to seed. Each day, I think about how I should cut them back and prepare the garden for fall, but I don't. In front of me the jade tree that decorated our wedding table is dying from rot. Leaves fall off each time someone bumps the table. We sheltered the jade on our journey to Oregon, made it a symbol of our love. It sat between us while we drove into setting suns. We hid it in the bushes that flanked our roadside hotels to give it fresh air. And when the temperature dipped, we carried it into the warmth of our rented rooms. Today I trimmed the worst of the rot away and repotted what is left but still the jade withers. Even if I had a bottle of Dr. Tichenor's cure-all, I doubt it would recover. The plant is too far gone to save, and I can't help but feel responsible for its slow decline. A man can lose himself to such wandering thoughts.

Jessamine County

1799

Daniel Boone is rumored to have said, "I can't say as ever I was lost, but I was bewildered once for three days." I make no similar claim. I'm more often bewildered than not. And lost. I spend hours trying to make sense of how Boone ended up living out his days in Defiance, Missouri. Come up empty. I know the details, the facts: debts he couldn't pay, an overzealous judge and a puffed-up sheriff, the fact that, according to his biographer, Boone "lacked the ruthless instincts that speculation demanded" (which I consider one further reason to commend the man). I'm also aware that the same year politicians chased Boone across the border, Kentucky named a county in his honor, and that some might call this ironic. But facts don't always tell the story, do they? They don't bridge that gap between narrative and meaning. The Kentucky Boone knew changed so much during his lifetime. By the time he left, there were more high roads and high bridges but far fewer high-minded men. And the buffalo Boone found on his arrival? They had vanished forever.

Barren County

1799

At some level it is the soil of a place that haunts. The elemental. Wendell Berry asked himself, "Why should I love one place so much more than any other? . . . What could be the meaning or use of such love?" I don't know that he's ever answered those questions, but he followed them back to the bluegrass. When we can't rationalize feelings, we submit to intuition; we make symbols. Of objects. Of people and places. But symbols, like names, can deceive. You might think that fear of lack reigns in a place called Barren, but here lies fertile loam that sits atop clay and stone and history. You can only know a place, its possibilities, after you sift its soil through your fingers. Wendell Berry also said, "What I stand for is what I stand on." So stand beside me. Look down at your feet.

Henderson County

1799

In Oregon, we stand on sidewalks that front boutiques selling terrariums and restaurants specializing in small plates. A man at the bar described my beer as possessing a "nutty finish with a bright head." What does this even mean? The naturalist John James Audubon (a dreamer bankrolled by his wife, Lucy) revolutionized ornithology by painting birds in their natural habitats rather than merely replicating stuffed museum specimens. He understood that the birds of America were most interesting when feeding and flying and fucking, so excuse me if I prefer to imagine us roughs in a place more like Scuffletown, where rendezvous end in broken bones that mend crooked, and where men and women wear their blemishes (my melancholy and truculence, your stubbornness and mistrust) with pride. We are learning to adapt here (there are notes of citrus in this IPA), but at what cost?

Breckinridge County

1800

Something of the ugly/beautiful lives inside us, and Kentucky excels in making the ugly beautiful and the beautiful ugly. Let us bring the sick jade to Tar Springs, where no one will judge its unseemly presence or think its poor health makes it less a symbol of love. Strip naked as Artemis did and carry the jade into the healing waters, but please don't treat me as Actaeon. I'll admire you in the light of a coal oil lamp but I'll not go to the dogs tonight.

Floyd County

1800

Even as I turn Kentucky into a lost colony of unlived lives, we talk about what lies on the horizon here in Oregon. We imagine such commonplace possibilities. We box ourselves into the expected. The happy couple. The happy family. And maybe this is just the course of events we are meant to take, the way lives unfold. What's the alternative? Tequila sunrises until we are paunch-carrying laggards? The weather-beaten life of the road? Even Jesse James couldn't outrun the bullets in the end. His eponymous son became a lawyer (how far the apple falls) who got his thrills portraying his father on film. It was a poor shadow of the renegade life, but maybe Junior was the happier man. The truer husband. The better father.

Knox County

1800

Step into the temple of Artemus and light this candle. Our temples are made of logs in Kentucky so be careful with the flame. Make a wish and I'll make one, too. Mine will be about looking back–a return to health for the jade, a return to some halcyon past–so perhaps yours should be about looking ahead. An antidote.

Nicholas County

1800

I trimmed the jade back to a single stalk with three branches–the tree a tenth of the size it was just weeks ago. I feel accountable for its decline. There's the practical reason, the overwatering of a caregiver given too much time and not enough responsibility, and there's the figurative, this sense that the jade has turned from a symbol of love into a symbol of lack. I've infected it (us) with petty want and selfish desire. If I could carry the placid stoicism of the pioneer hero or the Indian brave, I would, but I'm no stoic. Seneca the Younger said, "A wise man is content with his lot, whatever it may be, without wishing for what he has not." I confess: I am not wise. I am a hustler, a convalescent of courage, a–

Wayne County

1801

A sad fate: to remain forever wanting, forever praying for a different outcome. After a series of mishaps, an early group of longhunters carved into an ancient poplar tree the words, RUINATION BY GOD, but did they ever stop to wonder if the ruination came from their own hands, their own decision to hunt buffalo on land where they didn't belong, their supposition that rifles could protect them from both beast and man?

Adair County

1802

I've become the sort of person who prays away his problems, and though this capacity for delusion makes me weak, I've also learned the world is filled with surprise. In 1999 a Kentucky cattleman phoned a state forester about a chestnut tree along the edge of his land. It boasted uncharacteristically long leaves, teeth that curved inward, reddish stems. This is how we discovered one of the last mature American chestnuts. *Castanea dentata* is rare, having been devastated by fungal blight for most of the twentieth century. Scientists believe this particular chestnut survived not because of its strength but because it contracted a virus that weakened both tree and fungus. Isn't it strange how two illnesses together can help a thing survive when either alone would bring death? Sometimes I want to believe that you and I are that lone American chestnut, that we are survivors, but such romantic notions are full of hubris. Better the notion that I am the fungus to your virus, that together we might find balance and keep something alive between us.

Greenup County

1804

Scientists are breeding the remnants of American chestnuts (called "living stools" or "stumps") with blight-resistant Chinese chestnuts (*Castanea mollissima*). The goal is to make a hybrid that is fifteen parts American and one part Chinese, a nearly "perfect" tree that will survive if reintroduced. Schoolchildren have been recruited to plant saplings in Wayne National Forest, not far from where the Forest Service recently green-lighted a coal-mining project. If the trees mature, they will look like American chestnuts (only genetic testing could prove them false), but how does the one sixteenth of the tree that is Chinese chestnut feel about being trapped in a false body? Do either *dentata* or *mollissima* feel at home? And what is the natural habitat for a tree designed in a lab? Maybe it makes more sense to see this hybridization as a marriage–a coupling and integration of two lives, two pasts–a path forward.

Casey County

1807

The Puritans brought dandelions overseas to make medicine, colonists brought daylilies for spring color, and traveling salesmen followed pioneers west with lilacs, the smell of which conjured memories of home. We come to think of successful species introductions, like the lilac, as native; they grow to be part and parcel of our bosky acres and green rivers. The species that die soon after introduction (the bird of paradise in winter snow) are forgotten. But the species that threaten, the experiments gone awry (the kudzu and Asian carp), those we remember best. *Cryphonectria parasitica*, the fungal blight that attacks the American chestnut, was brought to North America at the turn of the century on a boat bearing Japanese chestnuts. At the time, one in every four Appalachian hardwoods was an American chestnut. Daniel Boone made beer and bread from their fruit. We know now, and in truth we knew then, that introducing foreign species poses risk. In 1890, Eugene Schieffelin, who longed to populate America with every bird mentioned in Shakespeare, released sixty starlings in Central Park. And because in *Henry IV* Hotspur says, "Nay, I'll have a starling shall be taught to speak nothing but 'Mortimer,' " there are over 200 million starlings in the U.S. Starlings that have laid waste to native bird habitats, such as the eastern bluebird and yellow-bellied sapsucker, bird habitats that no longer sit in the branches of the American chestnut, whose nuts no longer fall to the ground for us to make beer or bread.

Clay County

1807

I often ask myself how you would adapt to Kentucky. If I brought you here to the confluence of Goose Creek and the Red Bird River, would your coral lips turn alabaster? Or would you root yourself anew and flower? Become pregnant with health? Here's a dirty secret . . . Kentucky bluegrass is not native to Kentucky. You see? Naming a thing is a deception all its own. To deal with their incessant poverty, the people here renamed their county seat Manchester in the hope it would become as industrious as its British counterpart. It was sort of a last-ditch effort—like having a child and giving it your name to make up for the ways you've failed. We're always trying to make up for what we've understood too late. The Bible tells us this started in Eden.

Lewis County

1807

At the edge of the forest, scientists with shotguns and helium tanks fill balloons with pollen from the hybridized American/ Chinese chestnut and try to reestablish what was lost by floating zeppelins high in the sky and blasting away. If this is our best course of action, let us seek refuge from the madness. There are two islands along the Ohio, far from the buckshot, where you and I can live in peace. One island to make a home, the other to make a paradise. The bard said, "Love's best habit is in seeming trust," so lie with me as Eve did Adam, "and in our faults by lies we flattered be."

Hopkins County

1807

The American chestnut is monoecious, but it rarely self-pollinates because the female burrs turn fertile before the male catkins can shed their pollen. This is why the lone mature *Castanea dentata* in Kentucky is destined to be the last of its line. And it only lived ("acclimatized" is the word biologists use) because it suffered. Her burrs, then his catkins, lying barren on the soil of the Pennyrile–the timing always off, the same sadness year after year. I prefer to imagine those parts coming together to make new life–a copse, a grove, an orchard–and then, as the generations follow, a forest. Arcadia. The reality is not nearly so romantic. Those burrs and catkins decay and become peat buried in sediment. Then they are pressed dry and heated until every element save one is wrung out. In about four hundred million years, they become coal.

Estill County

1808

My point is this: Specimens in isolation are soon footnotes. Three summers before we married, I left you in Texas and retreated to the safety of Kentucky. I didn't know then what our future held, but I thought you might be the one to come running. Then summer turned to fall. After teaching my classes, I'd drive to where the mountains meet the bluegrass, the spot where Daniel Boone fell in love with this land. In Irvine, I fantasized over a FOR RENT sign in the window of a corner apartment, imagined us making a quiet life there, the sort where the deli-man knows your order and mail is addressed to a PO box. The apartment was rough, a fixer-upper. Holes in the floorboards. Layers of peeling paint. I imagined us on hands and knees (your hair tied in a red bandana) scrubbing the wood to shine. I imagined Irvine doing the same. The Mack Theater would take down the dog grooming advertisement from its marquee and reopen the doors. Midnights we would sing along to *Rocky Horror*. Weekends we would watch *Lawrence of Arabia*, your head nestled in my shoulder as you snoozed through the slow parts. They were all slow parts, you would say to me after, but you didn't say that because you were in Houston, lost among the millions, and I was in Irvine, playing make-believe.

Caldwell County

1809

Somewhere along my drive to Houston, I passed Needmore and Enon; somewhere I passed the point of no return–fearful but not yet enough to risk being the man who looks behind. In a Korean sedan I carried what I hadn't given away–clothes, books, a dog. I shunned interstates for two-laners, drank warming six-packs, and watched HBO in cheap motels. I gave myself time. To rethink this migration. To veer off course. The compass of the world was mine, but I continued south by southwest. In the rearview lay Kentucky (again). Always Kentucky behind, but never fully. I wonder if she's ever angry at my coming and going. I know that sometimes we burn ties to the things we cherish and call it sacrifice, but really it's just a means to simplify.

Rockcastle County

1810

Nowadays I return to Kentucky in dreams. When you are a muttering softness beside me, I am far away, preparing for your arrival. In these visions, I am a wielder of tools–a bricklayer and fencebuilder. I construct a place to protect us from some unarticulated anxiety–wall us behind a castle of rocks, stockpile saltpeter for guns, preserve food for winter. I build walls around walls, then look up nervously at a sky whose broadness screams vulnerable. Even the worlds I dream are subject to gravity.

Butler County

1810

Carl Jung said that as a condition to the modern condition, "we need to state things as accurately as possible," and that "we have learned to discard the trimmings of fantasy both in our language and in our thoughts." He saw the dream world as a remnant of the primitive mind, an antidote for our tendency to overvalue conscious thought. So let us be like our earliest ancestors and celebrate the elemental. In Kentucky, there are midden that prove how long man has desired this land. Generation after generation built homes atop the Carlston Annis Shell Mound, the highest point in the Green River floodplain. The artifacts date back seven thousand years. Midden filled with mussel shells, stone tools, flint. Pottery, hammerstones, and pestle. Fishhooks made from the bones of birds. The dead. Trust in your deepest instincts and come here to where the ground stays dry even when the rains come. I will build you a house atop all that came before, and one day, archeologists will dig up our bones and study them for clues about how we lived and why it matters.

Grayson County

1810

Houston was not sacred ground. Its beauty came from smog-filled sunsets and the blinking lights of oil derricks bolted to the ocean floor. Carnival islands at night. The city was built over swampland and falsely promoted by a pair of speculators as a veritable garden of fair weather, fine soil, and grassy knoll. The immigrants who'd sold everything to move there were forced to stay and fight the mosquitoes and yellow fever. And despite the odds, the city thrived. Like its cousin Big Clifty, the rails brought boomtown business, but Houston, unlike its Kentucky counterpart, had the ports when the trains stopped running. Six million strong by the time we arrived, so our trials were not nearly so dire. When the city flooded, we pumped the water away; when the heat became too much to bear, we cranked the A/C; and when the hurricane winds blew, we boarded the windows. A place tells you if it wants you, and Houston seemed disdainful of our presence. It always felt temporary.

Union County

1811

In order for a pair to be united, they must first be apart. Cleaved. And so a union is an accord–a healing, a matrimony. A complication. Houston was my sacrifice to you. Now you and I are cleaved in another sense of the word, wedded and subject to the other's movement. We ended up in Oregon after pointing to a map. We were still adventurers then. But Oregon has become status quo. Stable. I started teaching and you found a job and all of sudden we started slowing down when passing FOR SALE signs outside bungalows. A place chosen by mere happenstance, and yet we've never thought to question its permanence.

Bath County

1811

I recently applied for a job teaching in the town where I was born, and if I am wanted there, I will ask you to sacrifice your career here. I won't do you the disservice of pretending I would hesitate, that there is some doubt in my mind. The possibility of employment gives my homesickness a palpable end. But what will you do if this comes to pass? I am fearful of straying apart again, even if just for a short time. Call it a pilgrimage if that sounds better than an exodus–because life is not so hard for pilgrims these days. We can drive the highway east and live on blue Gatorade and Pemmican, sleep in hotels with sheets from Egypt and watch flat-screen TVs. And once we reach the salted waters of Olympia Springs, we can wash the dust from our skin and find each other and in each other, Kentucky.

Allen County

1815

Right now our lives feel stopgap. Half the week, I stand in an Oregon town two hours' drive from you. My work brings me here, though that's a sorry justification for the halftime apart. In the middle of the drive back, I pass the 45th meridian, the halfway point between the North Pole and equator, which is itself a halfway point and perhaps a truer one, though this is a matter of perspective. Halfway is not always as equidistant as it may seem. Walk south from Halfway, Kentucky, and you may find yourself in Tennessee, though how would you know you've crossed the border? Does one patch of woods distinguish itself so readily from another? And why does one patch of woods feel like home when another doesn't?

Daviess County

1815

Some nights I leave work and drive hours north through the fog and you are near to sleep when I arrive and we manage to recount only the most mundane details of our day. And some nights I am so primed with coffee that, after you've gone to sleep, I seek balance with a bottle of the Colonel's sour mash (a teeter-totter between extremes). I tell myself I'll get some work done in the blue hours, that I'll practice for that job interview, but really I'm just drinking to drink, letting my mind wander, and nothing good comes from it. Later, I slip foggy-headed beneath the sheets beside you and infect your dreams with whispers. I'm here. Remember me?

Whitley County

1818

Drinking is an escape and much of my idle time is spent considering escape. I hope you don't take this personally. My imagined adventures involve you, after all. You are a riding partner, my Sancho Panza, the brains of this outfit. The truth is I am a head-in-the-clouds kind of man—a conjurer of imagined life. A no-count, forget-to-feed-the-dog, forget-to-take-out-the-trash kind of husband. I could walk out our front door with you and look in wonder at Mount Hood or drive us to the coast and watch the waves roll, but I'm a poor guide to reality. I prefer to sit in my cave and pretend. I'll take you to Cumberland Falls to look at the moonbow. Do you see it shining down on us? Do you hear the waters crashing? Take my hand. Stay here in the nothingness with me. Stay in Kentucky.

Harlan County

1819

What we can conjure is often preferable to what we can hold. The truth of a place can sting. If I took you to the highest peak in Kentucky, we'd need a waiver from Penn Virginia Resources, which owns the summit. And we'd have to step cautiously because Black Mountain is unstable and porous, its veins having been stripped of their coal. This, by the way, is the company's justification for further dynamiting. The damage is so permanent we should let them finish the job. I'm afraid the myth of Kentucky I've created does not always bear semblance to the reality. I'm afraid that one day soon some executive will sign papers to blow the top off Black Mountain and our tallest peak will become Potato Hill.

Hart County

1819

We don't recognize our world anymore. When a wolf returned to Kentucky for the first time in two hundred years, she was promptly shot by a hunter who took her for a coyote. It took months of DNA testing to convince scientists the wolf wasn't a particularly large German shepherd. And while I'd like to believe the wolf was wild–that she somehow traveled down from the Upper Peninsula to reclaim the Appalachians–it is more likely she escaped a cage where her owner kept her hobbled and fed her scraps. I don't know what kind of world we're building, but it seems more vital than ever to fight against the decline side-by-side, to build our lives within a pack.

Owen County

1819

A friend told me that when a she-wolf's pups stray from the den and walk the long ridge toward new liberty, she calls out with a noise that is less howl than long moan, a plea to come back. But not all of them come back–

Simpson County

1819

Who howls for me? The stories we tell ourselves crumble if we pick at them. Pull the thread and the narrative unravels, and what was once true becomes little more than conjecture. Along the border, a small triangle of Kentucky juts into Tennessee for no apparent reason. There are no rivers or valleys to make a boundary, just fields and hills. No one knows precisely why this happened: the stories conflict. Kentuckians like to believe that one of their own fought for that piece of land. Tennesseans like to believe the entire border, except this triangle, chose to their state. And while you have to remember people from Tennessee are full of shit, neither story can be verified. The truth is that I've turned my back on Kentucky time and again; the myth is that somehow the land wants me back, which is hubris, of course, and ignorance. A place can't love me. Not like you.

Todd County

1820

If you walk the Highland Rim, you'll sometimes find yourself in Kentucky and you'll sometimes find yourself in Tennessee. There is no Rio Grande to separate them, no Great Wall. The border is a shadowland. It is not unlike my own nostalgia for home, which exists between imagination and reality, between sobriety and drunkenness. But the recent possibility of a job offers a tangible hook on which to hang my hopes. A border, so to speak. I walked outside our house in Oregon today, muttering answers to pretend questions from some faceless interviewer. I noticed the cosmos at the edge of our property had become brown and unseemly, returned with secateurs to cut them back (an excuse to procrastinate). One spindly stalk held a couple orange flowers, which I placed in a pale-blue vase. Last love flowers of the season. Last symbolic tie to Kentucky. I laid down a blanket of mulch to match the tidiness of our neighbor's yard and wondered if my mother had cut back her own cosmos, prepared her own garden for winter.

Monroe County

1820

Borderlands are fraught with tension. My dislike of Tennessee is part feigned, part genuine. I'll never order a Jack Daniel's "blended" whiskey. And I take pride in the fact that Kentucky didn't secede, that she doesn't tax a man who buys food to feed his family. But being able to answer trivia doesn't mean you belong. I've been imagining the sorts of questions I might get asked in the job interview, practiced wrapping my lips around terms like "pedagogy" and "hermeneutics," which feel false to say aloud. I'm afraid my answer to any question is really just: How do I get home? Which isn't much justification for hire. And the bluegrass revival slip slips away.

Trigg County

1820

I'm sure there are beautiful places to live in Trigg County, home to the Trigg County Ham Festival. The county seat is Cadiz–christened by a Spaniard and fellow nostalgic who found himself far from home. But let me speak of the interview instead. It was at a conference in Chicago. I sat in a stiff hotel room chair–exposed–and answered their questions, trying to figure out where to put my hands and whether or not to cross my legs, and who knows what came out of my mouth or whether my answers were all dreams of cosmos. When you asked how it went, I said, Good. (A lie I needed to tell myself.) A few hours later I was on a plane back to Oregon. I knew Kentucky wasn't going to be in our future, that I'd failed in my only real attempt to make this plea reality. Now I'm sitting at our kitchen table looking at the last rotting stalk of the jade. I long considered myself partial to plants and thought I had some facility with them, but life has proved me wrong there, as well. I cut the jade's last three limbs from the rotted stalk and repotted them in small containers with fresh soil. Then I chopped the last soggy remains of the jade to its base. Love in decline. When you walked by and noticed, you said, Hello, love stump. And for all that Trigg County might have to offer, tonight I'm just happy to be here with you.

Grant County

1820

The story goes that Pretty Boy Floyd robbed the Mt. Zion bank, stopped for lunch before leaving town, and tipped his server handsomely. That Jesse James survived a bullet to the chest and robbed a stagecoach on his honeymoon. My mother wanted to give me Jesse's middle name—a renegade's birthright—but my father insisted on the family legacy: Willcox. Son of desire. It's a better fit. And I'll try my best to make it work tonight, to give it life. Son of protection.

Perry County

1821

The committee in Kentucky hired another man, so there is no patch of bluegrass with our name on it. I suppose I could continue to imagine Kentucky as a twenty-first-century Shangri-La, but what's the point? It's coming winter here in Oregon and it's coming winter there in Kentucky. The university that rejected me, which aims to teach its students how to live with integrity, recently sold off timber and mineral rights to its research forest–a forest that once contained the American chestnut tree but is now surrounded by strip mines. And while I'd like to spin you tales about blighted landscapes returning to their former glory or pretend I was wronged by the hiring committee, I cannot sustain lies that forgive poor stewardship or a lack of awareness.

Lawrence County

1822

I am trapped somewhere on a bridge between the Kentucky of my mind (an idealized past) and the Kentucky I no longer know (some troubled present). I long for a way off this crossing, a third option between the extremes of reality and dream. Here along the Ohio, you can travel quickly between the towns of Ulysses and Lowmansville, between the imagined triumph of homecoming and the terrible recognition you're chasing an illusion. I am much more traveling salesman than wandering king, but I will raise myself up to meet you. I will try.

Pike County

1822

I turn to you, palms up. Lost, chagrined, a bit defiant. On a piece of bark I've burned our initials fenced by a heart: R+J. Before us Romeo and Juliet. Before us Roseanna and Johnse. Those are the types of love one should covet. Not the indifferent love of place. The grass and mountains and hills and rivers cannot hold me. The whispers in my ears do not come from Kentucky but my own deceptive heart. I have been spellbound, spinning tales to you, my lady in white. I should trust instead that we will discover our own fair Verona, our own Tug Fork, our own pinpricked love.

Hickman County

1822

I've proceeded with this plea as if there are constants, as if place (Kentucky) and person (you) are immutable. But one day you may wake and decide I am not the man you thought I was. This happens all the time. In Kentucky the landscape constantly shifts. Mountaintops are blown off and rivers change course. Once disputed Wolf Island is no longer an island, and though the courts gave it to Kentucky, it rests flush against Missouri. Even the ground we walk on, which we assume stable, can prove erratic.

Calloway County

1823

The literary critic Cleanth Brooks said, "We demand logical coherences where they are sometimes irrelevant, and we fail frequently to see imaginative coherences on levels where they are highly relevant." I am trying to say something to you through Kentucky, though I have reduced it to a symbol; I have been dishonest.

Morgan County

1823

Kentucky is merely a vessel to hold doubt, more pyrite than gold. In the Bible, the town of Ophir is a gilded port city, a place of riches that filled the vaults of King Solomon and sister to the mythic El Dorado, which spurred men across oceans teeming with leviathans and kragons. In Kentucky, Ophir is an unincorporated community where the post office closed in 2010 and the closest thing to gold is coal.

Oldham County

1824

In Kentucky, people who covet gold prospect near Goshen, where the wealthiest seclude themselves outside the smog of the city. But you and I have little use for gold. We covet clay. In Genesis, God told Adam and Eve to "Be fruitful, and multiply, and replenish the earth," though it's no longer the season for replenishing. Not anymore. The trees in Oregon are bare and the earth has turned brown. The garden is buried in mulch. And we are huddled inside, burning offerings in the fireplace.

Graves County

1824

What if there's no resurrection? Who will stand and speak for us? Who will don their fancy best and mourn our passing?

Meade County

1824

Neanderthals left their giant skulls in limestone caves, wildlings carved their initials into bark, and birds stamped their fossilized tracks beside trilobites lodged in sandstone. Believers dab themselves with holy water, and amidst the bathroom graffiti, next to the slurs and genital boasts, you will find initials or a simple: ADAM WAS HERE. An attempt at fact: EVE WAS HERE. Sometimes the initials are bound by a heart, connected by a cross.

Spencer County

1824

By all accounts biblical, Eden was a place of fine water and fruitful soil, situated along a plain or steppe. A *locus amoenus*, or pleasant place. Michelangelo depicted it as a grassy savannah with a broad, idyllic sky. In Kentucky, Eden is a mountain, much more in line with the poet Dante's garden atop Mt. Purgatory–a place to return only after one had walked through the sins they committed in the name of love. It was here, after drinking from the river Eunoe, that Dante prepared for his ascent into the cosmos, his meeting with virtuous b.

From that most holy wave I now returned
to Beatrice; remade, as new trees are
renewed when they bring forth new boughs, I was
pure and prepared to climb unto the stars.

McCracken County

1825

All I love in this world springs forth from that moment with the serpent in the garden. Soon man and woman brought forth the first warring brothers into this world, started our grand experiment. And children still seem to me affirmation that the world is okay, that it possesses a nobility worth sustaining. Children are a gamble, an act of faith, and there are many other ways of living falsely. The writer with his pen, the artist with his brush, the historian and his obsession with power. And then there is Speedy Atkins, who drowned in the Ohio River in 1928 without relatives, and was mummified by an experimental mortician. The funeral home kept Speedy in a closet, where he was viewed as a curiosity. Even the Paducah flood in 1937, which sent Speedy back into the river, could not change his fate. He floated miles downriver before being returned. Such rigid immortality–be it inked with words or swirled with paint or injected with embalming fluid–is no match for the beautiful uncertainty of the just born, for a future that remains open to possibility.

Edmonson County

1826

"Known" history starts at a precise moment, like the separation of B.C. from A.D. The known history of Mammoth Cave starts on September 10, 1791, when William Pollard sold a parcel of land that included the cave's entrance. Six years later a local man found the entrance, and a year after that, Valentine Simons carried out an "official" survey. But known history does not tell us history entire. Before it was recorded in books, natives used Mammoth Cave as a place to birth their children and entomb their dead. In 1812, men mining saltpeter found a woman entombed in the style of the Egyptians, a historical anomaly whose story remains unknown. The miners named her Fawn Hoof, and she briefly became known as "Kentucky's Posthumous Belle." At the Smithsonian she was dissected, though nothing about her past was learned. Eventually her remains were lost or discarded, as if she'd never existed at all. The other day you called down to me from the top of the stairs. I had my head in a book, likely some arcane volume about Kentucky, and I said to hold on. Hold on.

Laurel County

1826

By the time I reached the top of the stairs, you'd set the white plastic stick on the kitchen counter and gone on to complete some asinine chore, like making the bed. I called out to you and there, on the border of kitchen and living room, we clutched one another, laureled our arms, and somewhere deep inside you, cells (or was it clay?) quilted together and started to make a life—the size of a mustard seed.

Russell County

1826

How quickly elation gives way to fear. The questions spring forth. What if we're not ready? What guidance can we offer? And what exactly are we supposed to do next? These questions followed by promises: to do better, to be better. It begins with my declaration to join you in temporary temperance. We become a dry county: population two. Or is it already three?

Anderson County

1827

The radio says the Pacific Northwest is overdue for a massive, erase-the-coastline, break-every-bridge-in-town kind of earthquake. And it isn't long before I cross the county line and pull into the first bar and become a rebel yeller again. I'm just a turkey. A common breed. You're home sipping red raspberry tea, and reading articles on fetal development while I order another round. The negative space fills. Later, when I lumber in all boozy-breath and stutter-step, you read me the updates. Our mustard seed has grown to the size of a blueberry. A blueberry with webbed feet, hands, and a tiny tongue. I feign understanding.

Hancock County

1829

The only food you can stomach is waffles spread over with butter and soaked in sorghum syrup–food to keep the morning sickness at bay. We stock the fridge so that each morning I can place two frozen waffles in the toaster and serve them to you with decaf. Sometimes you vomit before work (so much better here than there) and I ask if there's anything I can do. What a fruitless question. Empathy, you say, that's all.

Marion County

1834

When sobriety fails, I decide to seek balance instead. A longer-term but muddier solution. In order to find balance one must first know the center of things. And soon we will be three planets revolving around what, exactly: Oregon? Kentucky? The child inside you?

Clinton County

1836

My anxieties, for so long root-bound by the past, now tendril out toward the future. Another word for possibility is uncertainty. We wonder what sort of child grows: Boy or girl? Priest or outlaw? Jokester or stoic? Carl Jung said, "Nothing has a stronger influence . . . than the unlived life of the parent." What a hell of a thing to say! One of our county's most decorated soldiers and one of our country's most heinous war criminals were both born in the Kentucky Highlands. The latter decapitated Union men and rolled their heads downhill. The former earned seven Purple Hearts and saved countless lives. Later he was denied a medal of honor because of a technicality-respecting judge. I hope, at the very least, our child doesn't grow up to be a technicality-respecting judge.

Trimble County

1837

The midwife glops a gooey gel onto your belly and there's a faint hiss in the monitor. I stare at my feet. Each day we do ridiculous things to make sure this all goes right. Lunch meat is microwaved. Hot dogs are shunned. Warm springs are generally avoided. In many ways we've simplified our lives to focus on the elemental, and yet our lives have grown fuller. The midwife probes, presses near your hip bone, moves the wand up. I feel it moving, you say. Sometimes they play hide-and-seek, she replies. The monitor hisses a faint static, but then, with the wand up under your ribs, the room trembles with the pitter-patter of a heart beating beside a beating heart.

Carroll County

1838

The heating unit of our house whirs on and off through the blue hours. Here I am. Wide awake. The dog snores at the foot of the bed and you are curled in a ball away from me, so I play big spoon and lay my hand atop your stomach. You told me I should speak to our child but I haven't gotten over the strangeness of it. Your belly feels to me as it always has–a belly. I've been hiding beer bottles in my basement cave, though I'm learning that just because a thing is unseen doesn't mean it's not real. Anthropologists study flagons left by ancient drinkers. Somewhere beneath my hand, arms flutter and legs kick. I wish I could express to you in these hours what I'm not able to when you're awake.

Carter County

1838

Nearly every night as you go to sleep (you are so tired nowadays), I'm at work in my cave. Fretting, scratching out words, dreaming. It smells faintly of mold and cobwebs hang in the rafters. The air ducts hum and the water pipes trickle and the concrete echoes at the slightest sound. A Kentucky of the mind. My cavern along the once-great Teays. Occasionally you hazard the depths to tell me goodnight but you never stay. It is cold and dark here. "Unwelcoming" is a word that comes to mind. And you have better places to be.

Breathitt County

1839

At night I've been watching you breathe. You take shallow breaths that I try to match with my own. Your stomach rises, rises, falls. Rises, rises, falls. It is wintry here, and no matter how much we raise the thermostat, the heater blows intermittent. When a cold snap comes, you curl into the sheets and pull them from me, and I slip out of bed to get a glass of water from the tap, look out the windows onto the darkness of winter. Tall brown grasses bend in the breeze, dead of all but spirit. The bed of cosmos lies bare, the ground hardened. A frozen creek of leftover rain slicks the sidewalk. I lay my forehead against the windowpane to feel the cold. When I return to bed you mutter, Where'd you go? Nowhere, I say and touch your arm. I'm right here. Waiting for first light.

Kenton County

1840

In my cave I read an account of Simon Kenton. As a boy he was a school-skipping idler. Never learned to read or write. Never much cared. At sixteen he fell in love with a girl who didn't love him back, so he knocked the man she chose unconscious. Then he ran away for fear he'd killed the poor bastard. What a childhood! Kenton paddled down the Ohio River, going by the name Simon Butler. He once saved Daniel Boone's life. Was kidnapped by the Shawnee and given the name *Cut-ta-ho-tha*–The Condemned Man. He later became a businessman and amassed a fortune (nearly half a million acres). Then he lost it all to men who had him sign his *X* to legalese. Legalese whose validity was upheld by technicality-respecting judges. Kenton was thrown in debtor's prison, but the people of Kentucky–ornery and protective of their own–lobbied until the politicians set him free. I like to think I have some of that same sensibility, that empathy for a man's imperfections, that mistrust of moral superiority. I don't identify with the methodical winners of life so much as the accidental losers.

Crittenden County

1842

Let me sip this pennyroyal tea and be honest for a moment: when I'm away for work, I stay up late with my friend the Israelite, who has a taste for vodka and midnight feasts. I have a taste for joining him. We tip our glasses and laugh, smoke cigarettes and jabber, tell dirty jokes and talk big dreams until we cry. I tell him I'm not ready. A cliché. He talks of the woman he loves, oceans away. And when the bottles are empty, I lie down on a cold, empty bed and think about what a mess I'm making.

Marshall County

1842

Before they launch into harmony, shape-note singers must collectively decide on a pitch. There is no middle C to guide them, no exact staff, and since pitch is relative, their song is determined by degrees of scale. Everything in proportion. Tonight I started a new book. Not some archaic tome about Kentucky or some quasi-intellectual discussion about the nature of longing and the flaws of memory. Tonight I'm reading *The Expectant Father: Facts, Tips, and Advice for Dads-to-Be*. It is a straightforward and moderately useful account by a man whose company I could not otherwise stand. I try to keep an open mind. I bend down and sing to our child, pretend your belly button is a microphone.

Ballard County

1842

I'm sorry if this plea has become more about forgiveness than Kentucky. Maybe it has always been that way. Maybe it is an apology for being so damned selfish. Me, me, me. I– I– I–. But what of Ballard, you ask. Well, I drove through there once on my way to somewhere else, bought a pack of Camels at a place called Cigarettes for Less, and crossed into Cairo. Is that all, you ask. No. There's more. There's a song about Ballard I remember from growing up, but it turns out the song has nothing to do with the county in Kentucky; it was a jingle for a West Virginia sausage company. Two cartoon pigs–one a farmer and the other a gentlepig–who danced and sang:

B–A–
double L–A–
R–D–S its true.
Ballard's brings the best to you!

That's what I remember.

Boyle County

1842

Our life is now newly filled with firsts. The first baby outfits sent from impatient relatives. The first furniture (a second-hand crib). The first time our child kicks so hard you gasp. The first time I lay my hand over your stomach and feel her kick myself. Hello, little one. I spend my weekends smoking pot and turning our spare room into a nursery with Allen wrenches and a Phillip's head. We sacrifice our dresser for tiny hand-me-downs from faraway cousins. In the corner, I set a glider. Welcome to the dollhouse. We find a rug on Craigslist–something soft for our child to lie on. The dog pads in and takes advantage, curls atop the rug and sleeps.

Letcher County

1842

The closer the nursery comes to completion, the further we travel from the headwaters of this plea. Kentucky fades. Our child is now the size of a pawpaw fruit but not nearly so fragile. I am coming to understand that there are parts of Kentucky not made for us. In *Night Comes to the Cumberlands*, Harry Caudill wrote, "Here the mountains were like the walls of a great jail."

Owsley County

1843

I must confess: I took that last quote out of context. Stretched the truth. Harry Caudill was writing about a Civil War battle when he compared the mountains to a jail. Context matters when it comes to the truth. Caudill was a lawyer, and despite his poor choice of vocation, he was honest about the challenges that faced rural Kentucky. Here's a little more truth: In Owsley County, government benefits account for over half the citizens' incomes. The average household makes do on sixteen thousand a year, and more children live in poverty than in any other county in the nation save one. This is not a place people move to. This is not a place the Realtor deems "highly desirable." This is where people cut and run, where they sell timber to make it through the lean times, and they are all lean times.

Johnson County

1843

Let's say you were to move here. Let's say my plea was successful and you were anointed the Belle of Blockhouse Bottom. You would be but one in a long line of Pennsylvania-born women to stake their claim in these parts. And many of your predecessors suffered. Take Jenny Wiley. While her husband Thomas was away, Shawnee and Cherokee warriors raided the camp and took Jenny captive, letting her live only because she showed such bravery while fighting to save her children. In the weeks that followed, she hid the fact she was seven months pregnant, but then the baby, soon christened Robert Bruce, came early. I realize this is not a happy story, especially given your current state. After he was born, Jenny's kidnappers placed Robert on a slab of driftwood and floated him downriver, and though Jenny swam to save him, she failed. For obvious reasons, I like to imagine a different end to the story. I like to imagine Robert floating along the sand shoals, gazing up at the moon and stars until he finds welcoming arms. I like to picture him as a young man, a guardian on his way to becoming king.

Larue County

1843

Lincoln was speaking of the Civil War when he said, “I think to lose Kentucky is nearly the same as to lose the whole game.” Even out of context, there is truth to his words.

Fulton County

1845

A man who spends too much time exploring a peninsula will eventually find himself on an island. Kentucky Bend is an exclave (population seventeen)–a tear-shaped patch of fertile land you must drive through Tennessee to reach. (Me? I'll take a boat). The Bend sits on an oxbow loop meander caused by the New Madrid earthquakes of 1811 and 1812, which also caused the Mississippi to flow backward and created, for a brief time, new waterfalls. On the Bend there's no church. No gas station. No one to tell you no. At the narrow pin of the peninsula, the pointed tip of the tear, the river presses against rock and wears it down. Wears it down.

Taylor County

1848

We shall not go to Campbellsville. I have no romantic visions for us where Donaldsons are not welcome. In fact, let me make a list of other towns we can skip: Disappointment, Fearsville, Ruin. And let us pass by Penile, too. Or better yet, let us drive by and take photos next to the sign bearing its name and laugh.

Powell County

1852

Every time I'm poised to set aside Kentucky, some complication arises, some halcyon moment of nostalgia. I have this memory, a fuzzy one I admit, of hiking with my mom through Red River Gorge and picnicking in the shadow of Natural Bridge. I remember it most because two old-timers mistook my mom for my older brother and said how nice it was to see the two of us out there in nature, like a pair of scouts. My mom nodded so as to not embarrass the men with her squeaky voice. It was a beautiful day. We had no time to accept apologies. Besides, I never had a brother, so they weren't wrong exactly. It was my mom who taught me to fish, to hike, my mom who taught me to appreciate these woods and their mysteries. That seems a heritage worth passing on.

Lyon County

1854

For nearly a year I've been trapped in an eddy, preoccupied with notions of home. I've leaned on nostalgia as a crutch to explain some black patch. One of my students wrote his research paper about alienation. He's a bright kid, thoughtful–prone to using metaphor to explain the weight of things. In the paper he writes of being homesick for Saudi Arabia, mentions a brother who was not talking when he left but is now "full of words." Most of the literature on homesickness studies immigrants. Here in the U.S., an Irish priest died of nostalgia-induced starvation, a Hungarian bride overdosed on laudanum, and countless others cut their throats or shot out their hearts. I want to tell my student about this rich history of homesickness and let him know he is not alone; instead I place a checkmark in the margins and write: "Good use of the personal anecdote."

McLean County

1854

It is spring again in Oregon. Crocuses and tulips emerge from hibernation, and on the warmest days, I take our three potted jades to the porch and let them bask in the crisp air. People smile at you on the street. Your pale skin radiates. The air around you seems charged with possibility. Over two thousand miles away, in Kentucky, a rough pigtoe ejaculates into the Green River and places his faith in the water's current; his sperm tumbles downriver until a female siphons it inside her. Above her, a coal barge chugs along the river's surface. Water bugs pitch in its wake. The mother lets the larvae bed down in her gills until she releases them back into the current to find an unsuspecting black bass or walleye. If all goes according to plan, the offspring will spend a few weeks in the gills before breaking free and falling to the gravelly bottoms to start lives of their own, far away from where they began. Here in Portland we walk with friends to get ice cream. And what a sight it is! You pregnant, enjoying a double scoop. God, this strange, wondrous place we call home. This world!

Rowan County

1856

Last night I dreamed I was a farmer and we had a daughter. We weren't in Kentucky, but in this Oregon valley. Our neighbors' hazelnut trees hung heavy with fruit and the air above their vineyards smelled ripe. Our farm was different–not quite ramshackle but not far from–the soil clay-bound, the timber rotted through. In the dream I was cutting back thorn and bramble along a fence. Our daughter helped. She was seven, maybe eight, wore a simple shift dress with a print I can't remember. She seemed like a good girl, pretty in her way. Smart enough to attend a nice state school one day, wise enough to settle for Bs. As I wrestled with overgrowth, a spider bit me in that same spot a brown recluse bit me years ago, but this spider wouldn't let go. I left our daughter there, rushed to tell you, but you grumbled in your sleep (was this a dream?) and suddenly I was in a bathroom–our bathroom but in Kentucky (though how could I know this?). Worlds spun. And where did our daughter disappear to? And why wouldn't you wake? The spider turned into a robot, released his fangs, and clicked away on seven, no eight, metal legs. Pus oozed from the wound.

Jackson County

1858

The Amyx family named Egypt, Kentucky, not after mountains shaped like pyramids or a river that flowed like the Nile or because they imagined their kids would grow to be sons and daughters of Ra; they named it Egypt because they felt as if they'd been exiled.

Metcalfe County

1860

In *The Book of the Dead*, all men must have their hearts weighed in the presence of Osiris and say before him:

I have not committed sin.
I have not uttered lies.
I have not purloined offerings.
I have made none to weep.
I have not pried into matters.
I have not shut my ears to the words of truth.
I have not multiplied my words in speaking.
I have not snatched away the bread of the child,
nor treated with contempt the god of my city.

The heart quivers. I grew up with a father who talked of responsibility and backbone, who held himself accountable. How far the apple falls. How far I've strayed, trapped in a cave of my own making, accountable only to my whims. I hear your footsteps above. In 1925, Floyd Collins followed trickling water into Sand Cave before it collapsed. For three days rescuers scrambled through the rubble to offer Collins crackers and water. A diminutive reporter from the *Courier-Journal* asked him questions, and the radio broadcasts made Collins a household name. On day four, the cave collapsed further and a rescue shaft was drilled. Famed doctor C. C. Howard was brought in to cut off Collins's leg and set him free, but the good doctor found only a corpse. "I never saw a thing that looked as bad," Howard said later. "And as hopeless. Never. Never. I managed to turn around with the crickets chirping and the water dripping and I crawled out of there."

Boyd County

1860

You call me out of my cave to light a stick of mugwort and hold it next to your smallest toes. This is magic to turn a breeched baby. When the stick turns to ash, I tap it on the side of a bowl, turn the embers red again, and switch sides. We go on like this for ten, twenty minutes. I enjoy feeling as though I have some use, enjoy kneeling before you and playing the part of supplicant. We laugh at the ridiculousness of it all as the smoke rises and fills our living room with an acrid refinery smell–a strange mix of a hash and scorched motor oil. I ask you if you feel any different. Yeah, you say, my toes feel like they're burning.

Magoffin County

1860

A month from the due date, my work ends, and I stop crossing the 45th parallel, that dividing line between us. No more half-time away. I stay north and we devote ourselves to the union cause. We attend parenting classes, though we are the bad naughty students who sit in the back. I put down *The Expectant Father* around Chapter 4–"Money, Money, Money"–and swap it for *The Birth Partner: Everything You Need to Know to Help a Woman Through Childbirth.* There's a section titled "The Emergency Delivery" that explains what to do in case I'm the only person around. I realize I'm closer to the renegade life than I've ever been before, that my mettle might soon be tested. And I want to be the sort of husband you can count on–the skilled frontiersman, the steady brave–but it is possible, probable in fact, that I'm more talker than doer.

Webster County

1860

A Kentucky poet named Cale Young Rice shot himself after his wife, Alice, also a writer, died. Rice wasn't especially noteworthy; he received little more biography than a couple paragraphs on a few websites, but each one noted that his "marriage was childless." This detail is strange–something so intimate in an otherwise scant account. Then I found these two poems, "A Charm to Bring Children" and "The Child God Gave." The first reads like an instruction book for begetting a pregnancy:

Take twelve leaves of the male palm
And write on each the name of a god.

The second begins with an imperative:

Give me a little child
To draw this dreary want out of my breast,
I cried to God

That poem ends with a stillborn baby and the narrator crying because the child "never smiled." So now the biographies make more sense. Cale must have felt so alone before the end. He moved away from his home after Alice died (grief of the familiar, I suppose) and into the Mayflower Apartments, where he shot himself just below the heart, which means he missed. And this last detail is so damn tragic it makes me want to scrape my eyes out.

Wolfe County

1860

Let there be beauty instead: White-haired goldenrod grows in one lone river canyon in Kentucky and even there restricts itself to rock shelters with sandy soil and only then at the mouth of the cave, on that border between sunrise and sunset, where it's exposed to wind and rain. Its yellow plumes flower in the fall but other times of the year it looks like a common herb—easily trampled and forgotten. Its leaves are so thin the print of a good book can be read through them. I mention the goldenrod not as some sort of proof that Kentucky is more magical than other places, but only to prove that existence itself is a sort of magic.

Robertson County

1867

More and more this feels as though I am writing an elegy.

Bell County

1867

An elegy for both place and time. An elegy for pioneers and Indians, for porous rock and wooded mountains, for the roughs and the want-to-be roughs alike. For the myth of this place I love. For reasons I still don't and never will understand. An elegy for boyhood things.

Menifee County

1869

A boy wanted to grow up but then he didn't, so he chose instead to dream a cave where he could live, a simpler time of fire and forage. But if you offer a caveboy a key to your house, he will draw himself a bath. Then the boy dreamed himself a dime-store western filled with gin-slinging gunslingers and noble treachery, but the western has always been lousy with lies. Jesse James was, by all accounts, a terrible person, and there's no honor to his name. Then one day the boy grew up without realizing he'd done so, and he was flawed and he cleaved to his flaws like badges of honor and his biggest mistake was to paint a world of opposites, a world with ladies in white and dark ladies. Behold the simpleton and his fault-making faults! Watch him compose visions! Watch him dream a boat, a bridge, a cataclysmic shaking of the earth. Because he's scared. Because he needs someone(s) beside him. Because he never learned how to make a fire and his cave is dark and lonely without you(s).

Elliott County

1869

Years ago you asked, If we had a baby, what kind of diapers would you use? I don't know, I said, Huggies? No, you explained, disposable or cloth? Here are some other things I don't know about: how to hold a baby, bathe a baby, change a diaper, give a good back massage, respond with the appropriate amount of empathy, build a career, invest money, pronounce the names of dead authors, fix broken appliances, and so on. I want to be up front about that. But a few things I can manage better than most: like cooking steaks and planting trees, like dancing wildly and catching car keys. Like making you laugh.

Lee County

1870

One day you walk into the sun and our unborn child shrinks into a ball. Vampire baby, you say. At night we tell her the names we're considering and ask for advice; we mark the moon cycles and bet on when she'll say hello to this world. Sometimes I play Otis Redding records and we dance beneath the stars. The three of us. In the mornings, I call to her, Bayyy-beee! Bayyy-beee, wake up! And she does. Together we watch her kick and squirm, this strange creature trapped inside you. We tell her that it is hot here and the garden needs water and that we are sweating through the night and maybe she should stay inside until I have a chance to install the window unit.

Martin County

1870

One day I go hiking with my friend, Chris. Chris is from Tennessee but I've managed to forgive him. See? I can be the bigger person. We hike to Punch Bowl Falls alongside drops that set the dog on edge. At some point my cell phone loses service and I worry about you going into labor, but in the end the water is cool and clean and feels right. I tell Chris my worries, and he says it would be nice to grow up in Oregon and that our kid is lucky. He nods toward the falls. If she likes nature, there's this. And if she's a city girl, there's that. And he's right. And I realize that for our daughter, this place will be home. And I want her to love it like I did mine.

Leslie County

1878

A dormant volcano overlooks our city, and at thirty-eight weeks, you climb it. We are attending a friend's wedding. I carry a small, useless gift. You carry a child. At the summit, you look on in disbelief. Where are the bride and groom? Apparently I misread the invitation and our climb is off by a week. What can I do but apologize? To the west, Portland shimmers in the sun. Beneath us, the earth boils. Just let me sit for a minute, you say. I do. Silently. The trek down still awaits us and the road has been closed for a bike race, and for a moment I want to blame this city–its stupid, healthy, bike-wielding residents–but the blame is mine. And you want to know what else? I'm not that sorry. Because you look beautiful atop this volcano–sweat-strewn and strong, hardy with pregnancy, a fucking cyclone of a woman. On the hike down, I lend you my shoulder to help bear the weight but it's mostly a futile gesture. Then I ask you to pause next to a road sign with the word bump so I can take a photo–a cheap but timely joke. The image is a tesament to your grace. You half-smile. This is our life together.

Knott County

1884

The branches I cut from our dying jade endure in windowsill pots. Their leaves are spotted and their aspect scraggly, but beneath the soil they've sprouted roots to hold themselves upright. I feel okay making a symbol of them, one that signifies this shift from two (RIP, dear departed wedding jade) to three (hello new family). The jades prove that everything is going to be okay, that we belong together, that we will carry on. On the birth plan there is one bullet point among the particulars that reads more like a promise: Father to stay with baby and mother at all times.

Carlisle County

1886

Everyone from the doctor to the midwife to the stranger on the street has the same advice on how to induce labor. Walk, eat spicy foods, and fuck. We manage the first two, walking by the summer's first cosmos on our way to the taqueria, and we are on our way to the bedroom when you tell me it's happening. There will be no sleep tonight. There will be a midnight drive to the hospital. There will be the mean nurse who I first thought was nice because she shared the name of my dead aunt, and later the nice nurse with receding gums. There will be a sunrise. When we started dating, we shared many long nights that turned into early mornings, bleary-eyed marathons of want; we danced ribald at sunrise parties, high on love and drug; we slept restless in bed and whispered, Are you awake? Uh-huh. Me too. So here we are. Again. High on a hill. You in a pool of water; me with palms pressed to your back. The morning sun slants through the window. You tell the midwife's assistant, I think the baby is coming. A little longer, she says, and leaves. The door closes behind her.

McCreary County

1912

A minute later, you yell, The baby is coming! The baby is coming! And I say, Oh shit! And you are reaching down into the water and my hands are diving down as well and together we lift this purple, wrinkled thing above the surface.

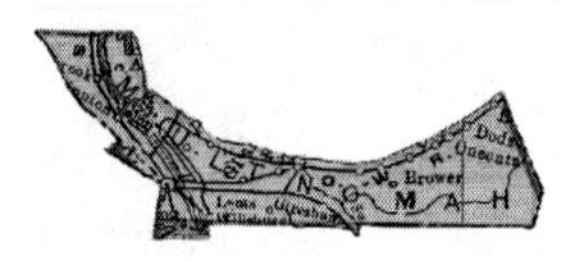

Multnomah County

20 14

And she screams.

A Note on the Text

While researching this project, I've been a broad, shallow picker of information and certainly not an exhaustive scholar. I've grabbed inspiration to suit my whim and fancy—equally reliant on Internet Message Boards as library stacks. I've sought story and myth as much as fact, though I've tried to be honest with the information presented in the book, or at least been honest when I've been dishonest. There will be people who claim I've erred. And some of them will be right.

Of course, facts themselves can be murky. In some ways, this book has become out-of-date in the short period between its being finished and its publication. For example, there is a reference to Russell County being a dry county. At the time I was writing the book, Russell County was, in fact, dry. However, in January 2016, the county's citizens voted to allow alcohol. Rather than revise the manuscript to reflect this change, I've decided to embrace the inevitable. Like all books, *On Homesickness* will become out of touch in its own ways.

Nowhere have I been more flummoxed than on the order in which Kentucky's 120 counties were formed. The sources on this subject conflict. I have based the order on documents from The Kentucky Department for Libraries and Archives and the Office of Land Development. The potential issues usually arise from a discrepancy between the date a county applied for recognition and the date the legislature passed a law recognizing said county. This proves infinitely more complicated than you can imagine.

More than anything, I want Kentuckians to know that I have not been just in detailing the wonders and charms of each individual county. This is most acutely true of the final ten counties, but it is generally true throughout the book. I learned countless wonderful stories about Kentucky's counties while researching this book, but very little of what I discovered found its way into the final manuscript. The crafting of a narrative and shaping a story took precedent. For that, I apologize. I encourage readers interested in Kentucky to travel there, drive its back roads, and meet its people. You won't be disappointed.

Acknowledgments

I am terribly indebted to the work of countless others, among them friends, scholars, and storytellers, including:

Derek Krissoff, Andrew Berzanskis, Jeremy Jones, Than Saffel, Abby Freeland, Jason Gosnell, and the rest of the team at WVU Press. Fellow Kentuckian, Danielle Delph, for the book design. Liz Parker and DHS. John E. Kleeber, ed., *The Kentucky Encyclopedia*; Susan J. Matt, *Homesickness: An American History*; Daniel Boone, *The Adventures of Col. Daniel Boon; containing a Narrative of the Wars of Kentucke*; John Filson, *The Discovery, Settlement and Present State of Kentucke*; the USDA; hauntedplaces.org; The *Oxford English Dictionary*; Ovid, *The Metamorphoses*; *The Book of the Dead*; *The Holy Bible*; Wikipedia; Shakespeare, *Romeo and Juliet* and sonnets 127–54; F. Kevin Simon, ed., *The WPA Guide to Kentucky*; Smog; Will Oldham; Elena Passarello; the *Louisville Courier Journal;* the *Lexington Herald Leader*; the *Daily Independent* (Ashland, KY); *Scientific American*; the *Los Angeles Times;* Joy Futrell; Tim Jenson; Royal Rhodes; Gregory Koehler; Mark Richard; Susannah Noel; Google; The National Audubon Society's Field Guides; kentuckysportsradio.com's county spotlight; The Library of Congress Map Collection; KET; Wendell Berry, *The Long-Legged House*; *Smithsonian*; Carl Jung, *Man and His Symbols*; Scott Latta; R. Berry Lewis, ed., *Kentucky Archaeology*; The Heritage Society of Houston; The Sierra Club; *Virginia Quarterly Review*; fishin.com message boards; The Filson Historical Society; Helen Fitz, *Mammoth Cave and the Cave Region of Kentucky*; my family: Martha Donaldson, John Donaldson, Emily Updegraff, Sarah Donaldson; the 2010 U.S. Census; *Missouri v. Kentucky* (1870); *Lapham's Quarterly*; Tim Shutt; Dante, *Divine Comedy*; Peter Rutkoff; roadsideamerica.com; rootsweb.com; Lewis Hyde; Ted Leeson; NPR; various baby development websites; John Keats; Rebecca Solnit on John Keats; the *New York Times*; *Murderpedia*; Kentucky Historical Society; Constantine Samuel Rafinesque; George Estreich; Jen Richter; Anita Helle; Jim Kiser; Edna Kenton, *Simon Kenton: His Life and Period, 1755–1836*; Armin A. Brott, *The Expectant Father*; Harry Caudill, *Night Comes to the Cumberlands*; Wendell Berry and Ralph Eugene Meatyard, *The Unforeseen Wilderness*; Jaber Almulhim; The U.S. Fish and Wildlife Service; Kyrnan Harvey; *Pass the Word: A Project of the Kentucky Oral History Commission*; Katie Hutchison, *Shaker Style*; Miranda van Tilburg and Ad Vingerhoets, "Psychological Aspects of Geographical Moves"; Penny Simkin, *The Birth Partner*; atlasobscura.com; poetrynook.com; John Berryman; Chris Bean; James Wright; T. Fleischmann; Maggie Nelson; Edison H. Thomas, "When the James Boys Rode"; The Kentucky National Guard History eMuseum; Mimi O'Malley, *It Happened in Kentucky*; Clark McMeekin, *Old Kentucky Country*; Roger D. Hicks, myappalachianlife.blogspot.com; Elizabeth Loftus's TED Talks on memory; Yaakov Schwartz; Svetlana Boym, *The Future of Nostalgia*; Linda Hutcheon, "Irony, Nostalgia, and the Postmodern"; The Max Planck

Institutes; Margot J. Vershurr, "Construction and Validation of the Homesickness Vulnerability Questionnaire"; Aja Gabel; Michael Parker; Nick Flynn; Robert Graves, *The Greek Myths*; *Vogue*; the countless fellow Kentucky ex-pats I've met in bars across America while watching the Cats, and, finally and most importantly, my family: Becca and Poe.

Jesse Donaldson was born in Kentucky, educated in Texas, and now lives in Oregon. He is the author of the novel *The More They Disappear*.